AF390328

MAYER SMITH

In the Arms of the Wild Hunt

Copyright © 2025 by Mayer Smith

All rights reserved. No part of this publication may be reproduced, stored or transmitted in any form or by any means, electronic, mechanical, photocopying, recording, scanning, or otherwise without written permission from the publisher. It is illegal to copy this book, post it to a website, or distribute it by any other means without permission.

This novel is entirely a work of fiction. The names, characters and incidents portrayed in it are the work of the author's imagination. Any resemblance to actual persons, living or dead, events or localities is entirely coincidental.

Mayer Smith asserts the moral right to be identified as the author of this work.

Mayer Smith has no responsibility for the persistence or accuracy of URLs for external or third-party Internet Websites referred to in this publication and does not guarantee that any content on such Websites is, or will remain, accurate or appropriate.

Designations used by companies to distinguish their products are often claimed as trademarks. All brand names and product names used in this book and on its cover are trade names, service marks, trademarks and registered trademarks of their respective owners. The publishers and the book are not associated with any product or vendor mentioned in this book. None of the companies referenced within the book have endorsed the book.

First edition

This book was professionally typeset on Reedsy.
Find out more at reedsy.com

Contents

One

The Forest Calls

The air was thick with the scent of pine and earth as Elara stood at the edge of the forest, the dense trees casting long, dark shadows beneath the pale light of the fading day. The wind whispered through the leaves, carrying with it a faint, almost imperceptible hum, like the distant echo of a forgotten song. It was the kind of hum that seemed to seep into her bones, curling around her heart, tugging at something deep inside her that she could never quite name.

She had heard the stories. Every village whispered of the Wild Hunt, of its cursed riders who traversed the realms between life and death, hunting those foolish enough to venture too close. But it wasn't the stories that had brought her here. No, it was something else—something deeper, more primal. The call of the forest itself.

Elara's fingers trembled as she brushed a stray lock of auburn hair behind her ear, her gaze fixed on the blackened mouth of the woods before her. The trees, their trunks gnarled and ancient, seemed to pulse with a life of their own, as though they were watching her, waiting. It was as though the forest knew she was here, that it had been waiting for her all along.

And yet, there was something in the air tonight that felt different—something charged, as if the very fabric of reality had thinned just enough for the unexplainable to bleed through. A sudden chill ran down her spine, and she instinctively wrapped her arms around herself. The evening was growing colder, the sun having dipped beneath the horizon, leaving only the faintest glow behind.

A low, almost imperceptible sound reached her ears. It wasn't the usual rustle of leaves or the song of crickets that would have accompanied the nightfall. No, this was something else—a deep, resonant note that felt like it had come from the very heart of the earth. The sound of a horn.

Elara froze. She knew the legends, of course. The horn of the Hunt. It was said to signal the beginning of the chase, when the Wild Hunt rode across the realms, sweeping up souls with the wind in pursuit of whatever they deemed worthy. But this was no tale told by children around a campfire. This was real. She could feel it in the pit of her stomach, the weight of it pressing against her chest, making it hard to breathe.

She shook her head, trying to shake the feeling. "It's nothing," she whispered to herself. "Just your imagination."

But even as the words left her mouth, she knew they were hollow. The forest wasn't just calling her—it was demanding something, pulling her in deeper.

Her heart quickened as she took a tentative step forward, then another, her boots crunching softly on the dried leaves beneath her feet. The wind shifted, carrying the scent of something unfamiliar—a trace of musk and the earthiness of something ancient and untamed. Her skin prickled with the sensation of being watched, though the path ahead remained empty, its shadows too dense to reveal anything beyond them.

She knew she shouldn't be here. There were warnings, old warnings from her grandmother, from the villagers, from every voice that had ever tried to keep her away from this cursed place. The Wild Hunt was a myth to most, a tale designed to scare children, but to Elara, it had always been more. She had always felt it, deep within her, that the Hunt was not some distant story but something inextricably linked to her family, her bloodline.

Elara had been raised on the tales of the Hunt—of how the riders came for those with cursed blood, how their fates were sealed when the horn sounded. But it was more than just stories. She could feel it in her bones, in the way her pulse quickened whenever she came near the forest's edge, as though something inside her was calling to the dark, calling to the Hunt.

And then, there was Finn.

She hadn't meant to meet him, had never intended to find herself tangled in his world. But there he was, a figure from the shadows, appearing on the outskirts of her life like a whisper on the wind. He was a man who belonged to the forest, a man who knew its secrets as if he had been born from its soil. His eyes were dark, almost obsidian, and when they met hers, it was as though he could see straight into her soul.

He had warned her, told her to leave the forest before it consumed her, but Elara had never been one to heed warnings. There was something magnetic about him, something that made her heart beat faster every time their paths crossed. He was drawn to the forest just as she was, though he seemed to carry a burden in his gaze, as though he knew the dangers better than anyone.

And yet, Elara had felt a strange pull towards him—something beyond the pull of the forest, something that had bound them together in ways she couldn't yet explain.

She took another step, the earth beneath her feet soft and yielding, as though the forest itself was alive, breathing around her. The trees seemed to lean closer, their twisted branches reaching out like fingers, beckoning her further. She had been here before, of course, but never this deep, never with the same sense of urgency. It was as if something in the forest had recognized her, as if it had been waiting for her to come, to answer the call.

Her breath caught as she caught a flash of movement in the shadows. Her pulse raced. Was it Finn? Or had the forest finally claimed her, its whispers now too loud to ignore?

The figure that stepped from the shadows was not Finn. But it was someone she knew all too well.

"Elara," the voice was low, deep, and carrying an unmistakable undertone of warning. Finn.

Her heart leapt, and for a moment, she felt both relief and unease. "You shouldn't be here," he said, his voice a mixture of frustration and something else—something darker. "It's not safe."

"I know," she whispered, her voice barely audible against the hum of the forest, the air thick with magic and tension. "But I had to come."

He stepped closer, his gaze never leaving hers, his eyes shadowed, as though a storm raged just beneath the surface. He was a man torn between two worlds, and Elara had always sensed it. He had warned her to stay away, to let go of the pull that was dragging her towards the heart of the forest. But like her, Finn had never been able to resist.

"Elara," he said again, his hand reaching out, brushing against her arm. His touch was warm, grounding, but his grip tightened when he noticed the marks on her wrist—the faint, almost imperceptible glow of ancient runes that had appeared out of nowhere. The same runes her mother had worn before her death.

"Why did you come?" he asked, his voice rough with unspoken emotion.

She opened her mouth to answer, but the words caught in her throat. Instead, she reached for him, drawn by a force she couldn't control. And for a moment, just a fleeting moment, they stood together in the silence of the forest, their breath mingling in the cool air, the weight of something unspoken between them.

And then, the horn sounded again.

Closer this time.

A sound so deep, so resonant, that it seemed to shake the very earth beneath their feet.

Finn's eyes widened, his expression darkening with an emotion Elara couldn't quite read. "We have to go. Now."

The forest had called her. And now, it was time for the hunt to begin.

Two

The Hunt Begins

The darkness of the forest seemed to grow thicker as Elara followed Finn deeper into its heart. The moon, hidden behind a veil of cloud, barely offered any light, and the air hung heavy with the smell of damp earth and pine needles. The path ahead was uncertain, winding between towering trees whose gnarled roots curled like skeletal fingers into the soil. Each step she took was a careful one, as if the forest itself were watching, waiting, testing her resolve.

Finn was just ahead of her, his silhouette a shadow against the backdrop of twisted branches and underbrush. He moved with a fluid grace that seemed at odds with the heaviness of the night. His dark hair fell around his face, but even in the murkiness of the forest, Elara could see the tension in his shoulders, the way his body was coiled, ready to react at any moment.

She felt a shiver crawl up her spine. There was something about him tonight—something that felt different. His usual brooding presence was now laced with an urgency that made her chest tighten. His every movement seemed deliberate, as if he were trying to outrun something—something that had been following them from the moment she had crossed the threshold of the forest.

"Stay close," Finn's voice was barely a whisper, but it carried in the thick silence of the woods.

Elara nodded, her breath catching in her throat. The wind had died down, leaving behind an oppressive stillness. The only sound that reached her ears now was the soft crunch of fallen leaves beneath her boots and the rapid thud of her heartbeat. She knew she should be frightened—hell, she should've turned back hours ago—but she couldn't. Something in her, something deep and ancient, wouldn't let her leave.

She glanced at Finn. "What's happening? Why do I feel… like we're being hunted?"

Finn didn't answer immediately. His pace slowed, his eyes darting around, scanning the shadows. It was like he could sense it too—the subtle shift in the air, the weight of something moving just beyond the edges of their vision. His jaw clenched as he turned his head towards her, his expression fierce, but his voice softer than before.

"Because we are."

Elara stopped in her tracks. "What do you mean?"

Finn didn't meet her gaze. Instead, he looked straight ahead, his eyes narrowing. "The Hunt is coming for us. For you."

A chill ran through Elara, and she felt as though the air around her had thickened to the point of suffocation. "Why? What does that mean? I don't understand."

Finn turned back to face her, his eyes dark, unreadable. "It means you're a part of it. Part of something older than anything you've been told. The Hunt has been looking for you—for your bloodline—for centuries. And tonight, it's finally found you."

Elara's mind spun, her thoughts scattering like leaves in the wind. She had heard stories, of course. Everyone had. The Wild Hunt. The riders who swept through the realms, hunting the cursed, the lost. But she had always assumed it was just that—stories, myths meant to frighten children. But standing in the heart of the forest, with Finn so close, his breath quickening, his eyes darting nervously, she realized how wrong she had been.

She swallowed hard. "You've known this… all along, haven't you?"

Finn's gaze softened for a moment, but it was quickly replaced by something harder, colder. "I didn't know it would come for you this soon. I didn't think you were ready."

"Ready for what?" Elara asked, her voice trembling. "What are you talking about?"

Finn stepped toward her, closing the distance between them with a single stride. His breath was shallow, his hand reaching out, almost instinctively, as though he couldn't stop himself. For a moment, his fingers brushed against her arm, sending a jolt of warmth through her, despite the cold that hung heavy in the air.

"Elara," he whispered, his voice low, almost a growl, "You don't understand. I should have stayed away. I should have kept you away from all of this, but it's too late now. The Hunt is already on its way."

Before she could respond, a low, haunting cry echoed through the trees. The sound of the horn, distant but unmistakable, reverberated through the very air itself. It was so close now, vibrating with an ancient power, the call of something primal and untamable.

Finn's expression darkened, his hand tightening around hers as if to ground them both. "We need to keep moving."

The tension between them crackled in the air, an electric charge that made Elara's pulse race, her chest tight. She wanted to ask more, to demand answers, but the look in Finn's eyes—the raw fear—held her back. Whatever this was, whatever he was so desperately trying to protect her from, it was bigger than both of them.

The wind picked up again, carrying the scent of something rotten, something decayed. The forest, once silent, now felt alive—too alive. Elara could feel it in the tips of her fingers, in the back of her neck, as if something was brushing against her, lurking just out of sight.

They continued moving, their footsteps quickening, the ground soft beneath them, making each step feel like it could be their last. The air grew heavier with each passing minute, as though the very trees were closing in around them. Finn's grip on her hand never loosened, his fingers warm and strong, but his body was taut, wound tight with tension.

Elara's breath came faster, and she found herself leaning into him, drawn not just by his touch but by the dangerous allure of the unknown that seemed to pulse from him. He wasn't just protecting her; he was part of this—part of the very thing that was hunting them.

"Finn," she whispered, her voice barely audible, the words slipping past her lips before she could stop them. "Tell me everything. Tell me why the Hunt is after me."

He looked at her then, his gaze a mixture of something fierce and vulnerable. His lips parted as if to speak, but before he could, the sound of hooves pounding against the earth broke through the air, unmistakable and deafening. The ground trembled beneath their feet, the sound growing louder, closer.

Finn cursed under his breath, pulling Elara toward a dense thicket of trees. He moved with a speed that took her by surprise, his hand never leaving hers as he led her through the underbrush. The sound of the riders grew closer, their presence undeniable now. There was no mistaking it—Elara could hear them now, the rhythm of the hooves, the wild cries of the hunt echoing through the trees.

"Run," Finn urged, his voice low and urgent, but there was something else in it—something that made Elara's chest tighten. It wasn't just fear. It was desperation.

"Why is it after me, Finn?" she asked again, almost pleading. "What am I to the Hunt?"

Finn's jaw clenched, and he turned to face her, his expression haunted. "You are the key," he said, his voice so quiet she could barely hear him over the roar of the approaching riders. "You're the only one who can stop it. But you need to understand— you're not just part of the Hunt. You are the Hunt."

The words hit her like a punch to the gut, and for a moment, she felt as though the ground beneath her had disappeared. Before she could process what he meant, the first rider appeared on the horizon, his silhouette stark against the moonlit sky. The horn blew again, closer now, deafening.

Finn's eyes locked with hers, and for a brief moment, she saw the truth—his sacrifice. Whatever it was, whatever bond tied them together, it was too late to break.

They were already caught in the Hunt.

Three

Whispers of the Past

T he sky above was a bruised shade of purple as Elara stepped deeper into the forest, the moon now fully hidden behind a clouded veil. The air hung thick and heavy, suffocating, like the trees themselves were trying to swallow her whole. Every rustle of the leaves, every snap of a twig beneath her feet, made her heart race faster, as though the forest was alive, constantly shifting and watching. It was in the silence, the way the night seemed to hold its breath, that Elara felt most vulnerable. The weight of the unknown pressed on her chest like a stone, and she couldn't escape the feeling that she was being pulled deeper into something ancient, something beyond her comprehension.

Finn had been quiet ever since they'd crossed into the heart of the forest. His usual words of warning, the sharp edge to his voice, had dulled, replaced with an eerie stillness that unsettled

Elara even more. He moved ahead of her, his steps silent, like he belonged here, like the shadows had become a part of him. She could see the way his shoulders were tensed, his body rigid, and the way his gaze flicked constantly from side to side, as if he were waiting for something to jump from the shadows.

"Finn," she whispered, her voice barely a breath. She had no idea why she had called out to him—maybe it was just to break the tension that hung in the air between them, the space where words once lived, but now felt impossible to reach.

He didn't answer at first, but his posture stiffened. He paused for a fraction of a second before turning back toward her, his expression unreadable. His eyes were dark—almost black in the dim light—and when they locked with hers, she felt a chill run down her spine. There was something different about him now, something darker, like the forest itself had taken hold of him.

"What is it?" His voice was sharp, colder than usual, but there was something more to it, a sense of urgency beneath the surface.

Elara hesitated, unsure of how to put the question into words. She had been feeling it for days now—the pull of something old and dangerous, something that seemed to echo in her blood— but how could she ask him if he was feeling it too? Or worse, how could she admit that she felt drawn to it?

"Finn," she said again, stepping closer, "What's going to happen? Why is the Hunt after me?"

He looked away then, his jaw tightening. She saw his fists clench at his sides, and for a moment, Elara thought he might walk away from her, leave her standing there alone in the dark. But then, in a voice so low that it almost got lost in the wind, he finally spoke.

"You're not safe here, Elara. Not anymore. The forest isn't just a place—it's a force, a living, breathing thing that draws those who are marked by the Hunt."

Her breath caught in her throat. "Marked?"

Finn nodded, his gaze still averted. He didn't want to say it, she could tell. But something was pushing him to the edge. "Your bloodline," he muttered. "Your family is cursed. They made a deal with the Wild Hunt centuries ago. And now, you're the price."

The words hung in the air between them, as oppressive as the darkness that surrounded them. Elara took a step back, her heart pounding in her chest. She hadn't been ready for this. None of this. The stories, the warnings, had always been distant, vague—tales passed down through generations, half forgotten. But this? This was real.

"You mean my family?" she whispered. "What do you mean, a deal?"

Finn's eyes flicked to hers, but he didn't seem to want to meet her gaze. He turned his back to her, his steps carrying him further into the trees. "It's not something I want to discuss. It's something you need to understand. The Hunt doesn't just come for anyone—it comes for those whose blood has already been touched by it."

Elara's mind raced, trying to make sense of the pieces, but the more she thought, the more tangled the web became. She had always known that something was different about her family— that there were secrets buried deep within her lineage—but to hear that the Wild Hunt had been waiting for someone like her… it made her skin crawl.

"Finn," she said, a tremor in her voice, "What does it mean for me? If I'm the price, if I'm part of this—what does that mean for my future?"

Finn paused, his back to her, and for a long moment, Elara thought he wouldn't answer. But then, he spoke again, his voice low, almost haunted. "It means that your fate is tied to the Hunt. You're the one who can break it—or seal it forever."

"How?" she asked, her voice thick with disbelief. "How can I break it? What can I do?"

Finn's fingers curled into fists at his sides, his knuckles white. He took a deep breath, and when he spoke again, his voice was strained, as if each word were a struggle.

"You have to go to the heart of the forest. Find the altar that was built centuries ago. It's where the deal was struck. It's where the Hunt was born. But I won't lie to you, Elara—no one who's ever gone there has come back."

She took a step toward him, her pulse racing, her breath coming in quick bursts. "You're telling me to go there?" She couldn't quite believe it. "But if no one has come back—"

"I'm telling you," he interrupted, turning to face her, "that if you don't, the Hunt will take you. You'll be part of it, just like everyone in your bloodline before you."

Elara's mind was spinning, the weight of the truth crashing over her in waves. She had always known there was something special about her family, something powerful and dangerous. But this? This was beyond anything she had imagined.

The air grew colder, the breeze picking up once again, and the faintest echo of a horn sounded through the trees. This time, it was closer, its deep call vibrating through the very ground beneath her feet.

Elara looked up at Finn, her heart pounding, her chest tight. "What do we do now?"

His eyes darkened, his jaw tightening. "Now," he said, his voice barely a whisper, "we run. They're already here."

Before she could respond, Finn grabbed her wrist, pulling her through the trees with a speed that left her breathless. The forest seemed to open up around them, the path twisting and turning, and Elara could barely keep up as they ran deeper into the heart of the woods. The air was thick with tension, and she felt the weight of something watching them, something lurking just out of sight.

Another horn sounded, closer now, the sound ringing in her ears like a death knell. The ground beneath her feet trembled, and she could feel the forest shifting, changing around her, as if it were alive, as if it were closing in.

"Finn!" Elara gasped, her voice breaking through the roar of the wind. "What's happening? What's coming?"

He didn't answer her. He didn't need to.

The trees parted suddenly, and there it was—the clearing ahead. But in the middle of it, standing on a stone altar, was the figure of a man. Tall, cloaked in darkness, with eyes that glowed like embers. The figure was waiting for them, as if it had been expecting them all along.

Elara's breath caught in her throat. "Who—who is that?"

Finn stopped, his grip tightening around her wrist. His body tensed, and his voice dropped to a low whisper. "The leader of the Hunt."

And just like that, Elara understood.

Four

The Price of Desire

The moon was hidden behind a thick cloud cover, and the forest had fallen into an unnatural stillness. Elara's breath came in shallow bursts as she stood beside Finn, her gaze fixed on the altar ahead, where the dark figure of the Hunt's leader stood waiting. The air between them felt charged, thick with the weight of something unseen, something powerful, and Elara could almost feel the pressure in her chest, as though the very trees around them were closing in.

Finn's grip on her wrist had never loosened, and as they stood there, waiting for whatever came next, she could feel the tension in his hand. His pulse was steady, but she could sense the undercurrent of fear running through him, the kind of fear that one couldn't shake, no matter how much they wanted to.

"Finn," she whispered, her voice trembling despite herself, "who is he?"

The figure on the altar did not move. His cloak billowed around him like shadows, his face hidden beneath the hood, his eyes the only thing visible, glowing faintly like embers in the night. The sight of those eyes made Elara's stomach twist, an instinctive revulsion rising in her chest. They were not the eyes of a man, but of something far older, far darker.

Finn's voice was low, but his words carried a weight that made Elara's heart lurch. "The leader of the Hunt. He is the one who controls everything. The one who decides the fate of those who are marked."

Marked. The word echoed in her mind, repeating itself like a chant. Elara's bloodline had been chosen long ago, bound by a deal made in shadow, and she was the one who would either break or fulfill that contract. She felt the cold bite of the forest air against her skin, her heart racing in her chest as her mind churned with the realization.

"What does he want from me?" she whispered, the question leaving her lips before she could stop herself.

Finn's eyes were locked on the figure, his face expressionless, but the set of his jaw spoke volumes. "He wants what's owed. The price of your bloodline. He wants you to claim your place in the Hunt, to become one of them. And if you refuse…" He trailed off, his words hanging in the air like a dark promise.

Elara's chest tightened, a lump forming in her throat. "And if I don't?"

Finn turned to her then, his eyes filled with something like sorrow and determination, and for a moment, she saw the conflict that raged within him. "Then he will take you anyway, and you'll become part of it. Forever."

A sharp, bitter laugh escaped Elara's lips, though it was more out of disbelief than humor. The thought of becoming one of the cursed riders of the Hunt, of being bound to the shadows for eternity, was too much to comprehend. And yet, in the pit of her stomach, she felt something else—a pull, a tug at the edges of her soul, telling her that this was not just some distant legend but a truth buried deep within her.

"What happens if I agree?" she asked, her voice soft, almost afraid to hear the answer.

Finn stepped closer, his body heat radiating against her. She could feel the tension in his muscles, the way he seemed to pulse with restraint, as if keeping something dangerous locked inside. He reached for her hand, his fingers brushing against hers in a fleeting touch that sent a rush of warmth through her veins. It wasn't enough to melt the chill of the night, but it was enough to remind her of the bond that was growing between them—fragile, but undeniable.

"If you agree," Finn said, his voice strained, "you'll become one of them. You'll ride with the Hunt. You'll be bound to its leader, to the darkness that consumes all who join. The Hunt will be in your blood. You won't be able to escape it."

The words hung in the air between them, and Elara could feel the weight of them pressing down on her chest, suffocating her. She had never believed in fate, never thought that her life could be tied to something so ancient, so primal. But standing here, on the edge of this strange, twisted world, she could no longer deny it.

"Is there any way out?" she asked, her voice barely more than a whisper. "Can I break the curse?"

Finn looked at her then, his eyes dark with a mixture of guilt and something else—something deeper, more painful. He reached out, his hand brushing her cheek in a gesture that was almost too gentle for the situation. "I don't know," he said quietly, his voice rough. "But I do know one thing. The only way to break it… is for you to give up everything you are. Your soul, your heart, everything. The price is steep."

Elara took a step back, her mind spinning. The thought of losing herself, of giving up everything she had ever known, was terrifying. But the thought of becoming a rider in the Hunt, of giving herself over to that darkness, was somehow worse. She felt like she was caught in a vise, with no way out.

A sudden rustling in the underbrush made her start, and she glanced toward the sound. It wasn't just the wind. Something—someone—was out there, moving between the trees.

Finn's hand shot out to grab her wrist, pulling her closer. His grip was tight, and there was an urgency in his movements now that hadn't been there before. "Stay close," he said, his voice low and controlled, but Elara could hear the edge of panic in it. "It's not just the leader of the Hunt you need to worry about."

Elara's heart skipped a beat. "What do you mean?"

Before Finn could answer, a cold wind swept through the trees, cutting through the stillness like a blade. The branches above them swayed violently, and Elara felt a sudden, overwhelming pressure in the air. The atmosphere had shifted again—this wasn't just the forest anymore. This was something far darker, something that had been here long before either of them.

A figure emerged from the shadows—a man, tall and cloaked in a heavy black hood, his features obscured by the darkness. He moved like a shadow, his presence overwhelming, as if the very air around him had bent to his will.

Finn's grip on Elara tightened. "Don't look at him," he muttered, his voice low and tense. "Whatever you do, don't meet his eyes."

The man stepped closer, his movements smooth and calculated, like a predator approaching its prey. Elara could feel the weight of his gaze even though she couldn't see his eyes. It was as if he could see right through her, as if he could see into the deepest corners of her soul.

"You've come to claim her, then?" the figure asked, his voice low and cold, like the wind itself.

Finn stepped forward, placing himself between Elara and the man. "She's not yours to claim," Finn said, his voice laced with defiance, but Elara could hear the subtle tremor in his words.

The man's laughter was dark, rich, and full of menace. "Oh, but she is. You've known this all along, haven't you? She's marked. Her bloodline is tied to the Hunt. She is ours—whether she wants to be or not."

Elara felt the chill of the man's words seep into her bones. She turned to Finn, her heart racing. "What does he mean?"

Finn's gaze flicked briefly to the man, and for the first time, Elara saw the faintest flicker of fear in his eyes. "You're the key, Elara. The Hunt can't be completed without you. But it comes at a price."

The man's lips curled into a sinister smile. "The price of desire," he said, his voice almost a hiss. "The price of what she truly wants."

The wind picked up again, swirling around them, and the air seemed to crackle with the sound of distant thunder. Elara could feel it, the weight of the storm building inside her. Something was coming, something inevitable. And she knew that no matter what she chose, there would be no escaping the price.

Five

The Unseen Pursuer

The night felt heavier now, the very air thick with the sense of something ancient and powerful lurking just out of reach. Elara's footsteps were soft against the earth, the crunch of dried leaves beneath her boots barely audible over the sound of her own breathing. The forest had swallowed them whole, the towering trees looming over them like dark sentinels, their branches twisted into grotesque shapes, blocking out what little light the moon could offer. The path ahead was a blur of shadow and uncertainty, but Elara kept moving, drawn forward by some unseen force, some gnawing need to understand the truth.

Finn was ahead of her, his pace steady, but there was something about the way he moved now—something urgent, something desperate—that unsettled her. He had been quiet for a long time, and Elara could feel the weight of his silence pressing down on her. It wasn't just the tension between them that had grown since they encountered the leader of the Hunt. It was something deeper, something darker, as if the very forest was closing in on them, urging them forward, making it impossible to turn back.

She couldn't remember how long they'd been walking, but the air had grown colder, the wind carrying with it an eerie hum, like a distant song that had long since lost its meaning. She pulled her cloak tighter around her shoulders, shivering against the chill that seemed to seep into her very bones.

"Finn," she whispered, the words barely breaking the silence. "What is it? What are we running from?"

He didn't answer immediately, but his shoulders tensed, the muscles in his back tightening as if he were listening for something—waiting for something. His hand flexed at his side, like he was ready to draw something, though Elara could see no weapon on him, no knife, no sword. Only his fists, clenched tight against the threat that was surely following them.

"You feel it, don't you?" His voice was low, strained, as if he were speaking through gritted teeth.

Elara didn't have to answer. She felt it, too—the pressure in the air, the weight of something stalking them from the shadows, just beyond the edges of her vision. The feeling of being hunted. It was more than just an instinct. It was as if the forest itself had turned against them, the very earth beneath their feet trembling with an anticipation that felt almost... alive.

Finn's footsteps quickened, and Elara found herself almost jogging to keep up. Her heart was pounding in her chest, each beat like a drum, loud enough to drown out everything else, even the faint rustle of movement in the trees. Something was there, something that wasn't supposed to be. She could feel its presence, closing in, like a predator circling its prey.

The air shifted again, the wind howling louder, carrying a strange, metallic scent that made Elara's stomach churn. Blood? She wasn't sure, but the scent was sharp, almost suffocating.

"Finn," she said again, her voice more urgent this time, "What is happening?"

He shot a glance back at her, his eyes wild, his face taut with fear. "We're not alone. It's following us."

Before she could ask him what he meant, the sound of hooves echoed through the trees—distant at first, but growing louder, closer, faster. The rhythmic pounding of galloping steeds sent a chill through Elara's spine, the sound reverberating in her chest. Her breath caught in her throat as she tried to make sense of it. The Hunt. But this time, it wasn't just a distant, ominous sound. This time, it was real. The riders were closing in.

Finn's hand shot out, grabbing her wrist with enough force to bruise. "We have to move faster," he said, his voice low and strained, barely a whisper against the growing sound of the approaching riders. "If we don't, they'll catch us."

Elara nodded, though the words felt useless now. What was

the point of running? Where could they go? The Hunt was everywhere, its reach extending to every corner of the forest, and no matter how fast they moved, no matter how far they ran, it was always there, just behind them, always waiting.

The ground beneath their feet seemed to shift as they moved, the trees twisting and bending in unnatural angles, as if the very forest was alive, manipulating the path before them. Every step felt heavier, as though the earth itself was reluctant to let them pass. The hooves were louder now, their thunderous sound pounding through the air, and Elara's pulse quickened in time with the rhythm.

"Finn!" she gasped, her lungs burning as they pushed through the underbrush. "What do we do?"

He didn't answer her, but she could see the desperation in his eyes. There was nothing left but the frantic need to escape. To outrun whatever was following them. But how? The Hunt was not something you outran. It was something you succumbed to.

Suddenly, the air grew colder, the temperature dropping so rapidly that Elara's breath fogged in front of her, like she was breathing in ice. She stumbled, her foot catching on a root, but Finn was there, his hand steadying her, keeping her on her feet.

"Keep going," he whispered, though his voice was strained, as if it were taking everything he had to hold it together. "We're almost there."

"Almost where?" she asked, her words ragged, her chest tight with fear.

"The clearing," he said, his voice barely audible, but there was something in it—something that made Elara's blood run cold. "There's a place. A place where they can't reach us."

The clearing. The words echoed in her mind, but they didn't make sense. How could there be a place where the Hunt couldn't reach them? The Hunt was everywhere. It didn't matter where they ran, what they did. There was no escaping it.

And yet, as they neared the edge of the forest, Elara could feel it—the shift in the air. The forest opening up ahead, the sound of the hooves growing quieter, as though the riders were being held back, as though something was keeping them at bay.

Finn's pace slowed, and Elara caught up to him, her heart still racing. "What is this place?" she asked, her voice trembling.

Finn didn't answer. He only nodded toward the clearing, and Elara's eyes followed his gaze.

The clearing was bathed in a soft, eerie light. The ground was covered in a carpet of moss, thick and lush, and in the center stood a large stone, cracked and weathered with age. It was ancient, older than anything Elara had ever seen, its surface etched with symbols that seemed to pulse with an energy she couldn't understand.

Finn stepped toward it, but Elara hesitated. The clearing felt wrong, like a place out of time, a place where things weren't quite what they seemed. The air felt charged, electric, and the hairs on the back of her neck stood up.

Before she could take another step, a sharp cry pierced the air. Elara spun around, her heart leaping into her throat. A figure stood at the edge of the clearing, cloaked in darkness, its shape indistinct but unmistakable.

The rider.

It was him—the leader of the Hunt. The one who had been following them all along.

Finn's voice broke through her shock. "Get to the stone!" he ordered, his tone fierce, but there was something else in it—a desperation, a fear that twisted Elara's stomach. "Now!"

But Elara didn't move. She couldn't. The figure in front of her, the shadowed rider, had locked eyes with her, and in that moment, she felt it—the weight of everything that had led her here. The weight of the curse that had marked her. The price that was about to be paid.

"Run," Finn said, his voice urgent, but Elara didn't run. She couldn't. The forest had claimed her, and there was no escape.

The rider stepped forward, and the ground trembled beneath her feet.

Six

The Heart of the Forest

The clearing was still and silent, the eerie glow that bathed the moss-covered stones casting long, shifting shadows across the forest floor. The ancient altar in the center of the glade seemed to pulse with an energy Elara couldn't quite understand—an energy that felt both foreign and familiar at once, like a heartbeat from another world.

She could feel Finn's presence behind her, his breath quick and shallow, the tension in his shoulders palpable. His hand hovered at her back, a constant reminder that he was here, but even his warmth did little to ease the cold that had settled deep within her bones. The wind had died down, and the usual sounds of the forest—distant birdcalls, rustling leaves—were gone, replaced by an oppressive silence that made every footstep, every breath, feel like a violation.

She stood frozen at the edge of the clearing, unable to move, as the figure of the Hunt's leader slowly approached. His cloak swirled around him like smoke, his hood drawn low over his face, leaving only the faintest glow of his eyes visible in the darkness. They were like twin embers, burning with a light that seemed to come from within, a light that was both inviting and terrifying.

Elara's heart thudded in her chest as the rider stepped forward, his presence heavier with each passing second. She wanted to look away, to turn and run, but she couldn't. It was as though his gaze was a force in itself, a magnetic pull that kept her rooted to the spot.

"Elara," the voice came from the rider, low and reverberating with an ancient power. It was the same voice she had heard in the shadows, in her dreams, the voice that had haunted her every step since she'd first entered this cursed forest. But now, it was closer, more real, and it made her skin crawl. "The time has come."

The words hung in the air, heavy with meaning. Elara's pulse raced, her mind scrambling to make sense of what was happening. She had always known, deep down, that this was where it would lead. The forest had been calling her, guiding her toward this moment, but now that it had arrived, she was not sure she was ready to face it.

Finn stepped forward, his body blocking hers instinctively. His hand rested on the hilt of a blade that was not there—he was unarmed—but his posture was that of a man who had long ago accepted that some battles could not be fought with weapons.

"You will not have her," he growled, his voice strained with the kind of restraint Elara had never heard before. There was something different about him, something that hinted at the battle he was fighting deep inside. She had seen it in his eyes before—an internal war that threatened to tear him apart—and now, it was clear that whatever was coming, he wasn't going to let it take her without a fight.

The Hunt's leader did not flinch. His gaze moved slowly from Finn to Elara, and in that moment, she felt as if she were being measured, as if she were a mere object to be weighed and judged. His eyes burned with an intensity that made her breath catch, and she instinctively stepped back, her heart racing, but Finn's grip on her arm held her steady.

"You cannot escape your fate, Elara," the leader's voice continued, cold and relentless. "Your bloodline has already made the choice for you. You are bound to the Hunt now—whether you accept it or not."

Elara's chest tightened, the words settling like stones in her stomach. Bound to the Hunt. It was what she had feared all along, but hearing it spoken aloud, with such finality, was like a death sentence. She wanted to argue, to scream, to refuse, but the words caught in her throat. The weight of her family's curse was too heavy, too old. There was nothing she could say that would change the course that had already been set.

"You're lying," Elara whispered, her voice shaking, barely able to meet the leader's eyes. "I don't want this. I won't be part of this."

A low, mocking laugh escaped the leader. It echoed through the clearing, sending a shiver down her spine. "You don't have a choice. The Hunt does not ask for permission. It does not wait for your consent. It simply takes what is owed."

Finn's hand tightened around her arm, but there was no anger in his grip—only an unspoken plea. He knew, as much as she did, that there was nothing more they could do.

The ground beneath them seemed to shift, the earth trembling with the weight of the Hunt's presence, as if it were a living thing, shifting with anticipation. A cold breeze picked up, rustling the leaves in the trees above, and Elara instinctively reached for Finn's hand, her fingers brushing his, seeking the only warmth she had left in this frozen, alien world. His fingers squeezed hers, the gesture firm but not enough to bring comfort. She could feel his heart racing against his chest, just as hers did, but there was something in his eyes—something raw, something vulnerable—that stopped her breath.

"I won't let it take you," Finn said, his voice fierce, but the desperation in it was unmistakable. "I swear it."

The leader's gaze shifted to Finn, and for a moment, Elara thought she saw something like amusement in those burning eyes. "You think you can protect her?" the leader mused, his voice low and taunting. "You think you can stop what's already been set in motion? You're nothing more than a fleeting shadow, a whisper in the wind. The Hunt is eternal. It cannot be stopped."

Elara felt a surge of panic, her pulse racing, her chest tight with the weight of the realization. She couldn't outrun this. She couldn't hide from it. The Hunt was part of her, part of who she was, and no matter how much she wished it away, it would always be there, just out of sight, waiting for the moment to claim her.

"You're wrong," Elara said, her voice breaking free, sharper now. "I am not part of your Hunt. I will not let it control me. I will fight."

The leader's eyes gleamed, a dark amusement flickering behind them. "You fight, but it won't matter. In the end, you will belong to us. And once you do, there will be no escaping."

Before Elara could respond, the air around them grew colder, the temperature dropping so suddenly that she could see her breath forming in front of her, thick and visible in the air. The trees seemed to lean in, their branches creaking and groaning, like the forest itself was drawing in a breath, waiting for something.

Finn's grip on her hand tightened. "We need to go," he said urgently, his voice low, though his gaze never left the leader. "Now."

Elara felt a surge of defiance rise up within her, but she knew, deep down, that Finn was right. They had no choice. The leader was more than just a man. He was something far older, far more dangerous. And Elara knew, in that moment, that there was no escaping the Hunt—not without paying the price.

But she wouldn't go quietly. She couldn't. Not now.

Finn pulled her back, urging her toward the edge of the clearing, his hand still gripping hers, but Elara hesitated. The leader's voice echoed in her mind, a haunting whisper in the back of her thoughts.

"You will come to us, Elara," he said, his tone slow, deliberate. "The Hunt will claim what is owed. There is no escape."

Elara closed her eyes, the weight of his words pressing down on her, but she refused to let them break her. She wouldn't let the Hunt take her without a fight.

With one last, lingering look at the figure in the clearing, Elara turned away, letting Finn lead her through the trees, back into the shadowed forest. The Hunt was closer now, and Elara could feel its cold breath on her neck, but as long as she was with Finn, she still had a chance.

A chance to break free.

Seven

Ties That Bind

The wind howled through the trees, its mournful cry echoing across the dark expanse of the forest as Elara and Finn moved deeper into its shadowed heart. The underbrush was thick, the ground uneven beneath their feet, yet they moved with purpose, each step fueled by the growing urgency to escape the presence that had been stalking them.

Elara's breath came in quick, shallow bursts as she struggled to keep up. Finn's pace was relentless, and despite the burning in her lungs, she had no choice but to follow. The air felt thick, charged with the forest's energy, as if the very earth beneath her feet was holding its breath, waiting for something to happen.

Her heart hammered in her chest, and her mind raced with the weight of the events unfolding around them. The leader of the Hunt—the figure cloaked in darkness—was not just a shadow from some ancient tale. He was real, and the Hunt was real, and Elara had no idea how much longer they could outrun it.

Finn's grip on her wrist tightened, pulling her forward when she stumbled, his touch burning even through the layers of fabric that separated them. She glanced up at him, and for the first time in what felt like forever, their eyes met. There was a desperation in his gaze, a silent plea that made Elara's chest tighten with a feeling she couldn't quite name.

"Finn, where are we going?" she whispered, her voice trembling as they pushed forward.

He didn't answer immediately, his jaw set in a hard line as he glanced over his shoulder. His movements were sharp, calculated, as if he were expecting something to emerge from the trees at any moment. Elara could feel it too—the sense of something closing in, the sensation of being hunted. But there was no sound, no sign of movement other than the wind that whipped through the branches overhead.

"We're heading to the edge of the forest," Finn said at last, his voice strained. "There's a place I know. A place where we might be able to lose them."

The words were meant to reassure her, but Elara felt only a growing unease. The Hunt didn't just lose track of its prey. It followed, relentlessly, and no matter how far they ran, the darkness would be there, just behind them.

"What if they're already there?" Elara asked, though she already knew the answer. It was a question born of fear, of the cold realization that no matter where they went, they were still trapped in the web of fate.

"They won't be," Finn said, though his voice was tight, and there was something in his eyes that made Elara uneasy. It wasn't just fear—it was something darker, something he hadn't told her, a secret that hung between them like a barrier. She wanted to press him, to ask him what he was holding back, but the words died in her throat.

Ahead, the trees began to thin, the thick canopy of leaves opening up to reveal a small, hidden clearing. The moonlight filtered down through the branches, casting a silver glow across the moss-covered stones that littered the ground. The clearing was eerily quiet, the sounds of the forest's creatures fading into nothingness as they approached.

Finn slowed as they entered, his body tense, his eyes scanning the edges of the clearing. The air felt different here—still, almost oppressive. Elara could feel the weight of it pressing down on her chest, as though the very forest were holding its breath. She shivered involuntarily, her senses heightened as she tried to make sense of the stillness around them.

"What is this place?" Elara asked, stepping into the center of the clearing. She could feel the magic in the air, an ancient, pulsing energy that seemed to seep into her very skin. The ground beneath her feet was solid, but there was something else—something alive—that she couldn't quite put her finger on.

"It's an old place," Finn said, his voice low and guarded. "A place of power. My family used to come here. There's a ward here—a protection that should keep them away, at least for a time."

Elara nodded slowly, though she wasn't sure she believed him. The ward sounded too easy, too simple. If there was one thing she had learned since stepping foot in this cursed forest, it was that nothing was as it seemed. The Hunt had a way of twisting the truth, of manipulating reality itself.

Suddenly, a sharp crack echoed through the trees, the sound of a branch snapping. Elara froze, her heart leaping into her throat. She didn't need to look at Finn to know that he had heard it too. His muscles tensed, his hand moving instinctively to her side, as though to shield her from whatever danger approached.

"Stay close," he whispered, his voice tight with urgency.

Elara did as he said, stepping closer to him, the warmth of his body a sharp contrast to the cold, damp air that surrounded them. The silence had returned, but it was the kind of silence that came before a storm—unnerving, pregnant with anticipation.

They waited. The seconds stretched into what felt like hours, the tension between them building, coiling like a spring ready to snap.

And then, without warning, the figure stepped into the clearing.

It was a man, tall and cloaked in shadows, his face hidden

beneath the deep folds of his hood. He moved with the same unnatural grace that Elara had seen in the leader of the Hunt, his every step calculated, deliberate. His presence seemed to twist the air around him, bending reality in a way that made Elara's skin crawl.

Finn's hand tightened around hers, his grip so strong that it almost hurt. "We have to go," he hissed through gritted teeth. "Now."

But Elara didn't move. She couldn't. There was something about the figure that kept her rooted to the spot, a magnetic pull that she couldn't ignore.

"Who are you?" she demanded, her voice trembling but defiant.

The figure didn't answer immediately. He simply watched her, his eyes glowing faintly beneath the hood, like twin embers in the darkness. There was something unsettlingly familiar about the way he looked at her—something that sent a shiver down her spine.

"You know who I am," the figure said at last, his voice low and cold. "I am a shadow of the Hunt, one of its many hunters. And I have come for you, Elara."

Elara's breath caught in her throat, her pulse spiking at the mention of her name. This was no ordinary man. This was one of the riders, one of the figures who had been hunting her from the moment she had set foot in the forest. She felt a wave of nausea wash over her as the reality of the situation hit her.

There was no escape. The Hunt had already claimed her.

Finn stepped in front of her, his body a shield, his eyes flashing with anger and fear. "You won't take her," he spat, his voice sharp.

The rider chuckled, the sound cold and mocking. "You think you can protect her? You are nothing, just a man caught in a game far beyond your control."

Elara could see the truth in the rider's words, though she hated to admit it. The Hunt was an ancient force, one that had claimed countless lives over the centuries. And now, it had come for her.

"No," Finn said, his voice trembling with raw emotion. "I'll protect her. I'll die before I let the Hunt take her."

Elara's heart lurched at his words. She wanted to say something, wanted to tell him to stop, to run, to leave before it was too late, but the words stuck in her throat. She couldn't let him do this for her. Not again.

The rider took a step closer, his eyes glowing brighter now, burning with a dangerous intensity. "You are too late," he said, his voice dark with finality. "The Hunt does not wait for you to make a choice. The price has already been paid."

Finn drew in a breath, his body trembling with the effort to hold himself back. Elara could see the war raging inside him, the desire to protect her warring with the knowledge that they had no way out.

And then, without warning, Finn turned to face her, his hand reaching out to cup her face, his thumb brushing over her cheek in a gesture so tender it took her breath away. "Whatever happens," he whispered, his voice hoarse with emotion, "I love you."

The words hit her like a wave, crashing over her and sweeping her into a sea of conflicting emotions. The weight of them was too much, and for a moment, she couldn't breathe, couldn't think.

But then, with a surge of strength, Elara tore herself away from him, her hand gripping his with a force she didn't know she had. "No," she said, her voice shaking but resolute. "We don't have to do this. We can fight. We can escape."

Finn's eyes softened with pain, but there was something else there too—something like hope, like the fragile promise of something better.

And for a brief, fleeting moment, Elara believed him.

But then the rider moved forward, and all hope seemed to slip through her fingers like sand.

Eight

Betrayal's Kiss

The air in the clearing was thick with tension, suffocating in its intensity. The wind had died down again, leaving only the eerie sounds of the forest—a distant rustling, the sharp snap of a twig, the occasional hoot of an owl—each noise amplified in the unnatural stillness. Elara's breath came in ragged gasps as she stood at the edge of the clearing, Finn at her side. The figure, the rider of the Hunt, was still there, his form barely visible beneath the swirling cloak of shadows that surrounded him. He hadn't moved since he stepped into the clearing, but Elara could feel his gaze, sharp and unyielding, drilling into her.

She couldn't look away.

The glow from the rider's eyes flickered like embers in the night, casting faint light over his face, but the rest of his features remained hidden in shadow. His presence was like a weight, pressing down on her chest, making it harder and harder to breathe. There was something unsettlingly familiar about him, though she couldn't place it. It was as though he had been a part of her life for far longer than she realized, a piece of her past she had forgotten or buried too deeply to recall.

And then, Finn's voice broke the silence.

"Elara, stay behind me," he whispered, his words rough with desperation. But she could hear the undercurrent of something else in his tone, something darker. A warning.

For the briefest moment, Elara glanced at him, her heart sinking as she saw the determination in his eyes—the same determination that had drawn her to him in the first place, the same look he had given her when he promised to protect her, no matter the cost. But now, something had changed in him. There was a shadow behind his gaze, a flicker of something unspoken, something that chilled her to her very core.

Before she could ask him what he meant, the rider took a step forward, his cloak swirling around him like the dark tide of the night, and he spoke in a voice that echoed through the clearing, sharp and hollow.

"Do you think you can protect her, Finn?" The rider's words dripped with disdain, like venom laced with truth. "She is already ours. The bond is forged, the pact made. You cannot change what is already written."

Finn's body went rigid, but he didn't move. "You're wrong," he spat, his voice tight with anger. "I won't let you take her."

Elara's heart thundered in her chest as she watched the exchange, unable to tear her gaze away from the rider. She felt something shift within her, something dark and powerful rising to the surface. This wasn't just about her anymore. It wasn't just about the curse or the Hunt. It was about Finn, too. He was so fiercely protective of her, but she had begun to sense that there was something he was holding back—something that he wasn't telling her.

The rider chuckled, a cold, mocking sound that made Elara's skin crawl. "You still think you can save her? You have no power here, Finn. Not anymore."

Elara felt the truth in his words. The weight of the curse was too much. It had been there from the beginning, a shadow that had followed her through her entire life. She had been born for this, marked by it. The path she walked had already been chosen, whether she accepted it or not.

But she couldn't bring herself to believe that. Not after everything she had shared with Finn. Not after the way he had looked at her, the way his touch had burned through her, the way she had felt a bond form between them that couldn't be explained by any curse or pact.

She stepped forward, ignoring Finn's warning as she walked closer to the rider. Her heart was pounding, but her feet moved with a will of their own. The rider's gaze followed her, those ember-like eyes glowing brighter as she approached.

"I won't be part of this," she said, her voice steady despite the turmoil swirling inside her. "I won't let it control me. I will not be part of your Hunt. I choose my own path."

The rider's lips curled into a smile that was more a sneer than anything else. "You think you have a choice? You think you can defy the Hunt? There is no escaping it. You will join us, one way or another."

Her chest tightened at the rider's words, but she didn't let the fear show. She looked back at Finn, but instead of finding reassurance in his eyes, she saw something else. Something darker. His gaze flickered briefly to the rider, his expression unreadable, and then he looked at her—really looked at her— and in that moment, Elara felt as if she were seeing him for the first time.

There was a shift in the air, subtle but undeniable. A chill that was not caused by the wind, a shift that settled between them, heavy and suffocating. Finn's expression changed, something cold flickering across his face. His lips parted as if to speak, but the words didn't come.

"Elara," he whispered, his voice tight. "I need you to listen to me."

She nodded, though the unease gnawing at her only grew stronger.

"You can't escape this," Finn continued, his voice raw, as if something deep inside him were unraveling. "There's a reason you were brought here. A reason your bloodline is tied to the Hunt. I tried to protect you from it. I tried to keep you safe. But I was wrong."

Her heart stopped at his words, her breath catching in her throat. "What do you mean? What are you saying, Finn?"

The pain in his eyes was unmistakable. "I'm the one who bound you to the Hunt," he confessed, his voice breaking with the weight of the truth. "I'm the reason you're marked."

The world around her seemed to spin, and for a moment, she thought she might fall. Her knees weakened, but she held herself upright, though she could feel the tremor in her hands, the rush of disbelief crashing over her like a tidal wave. The words he spoke—his confession—felt like an anchor that threatened to drag her under.

"You—what?" she breathed, her voice barely more than a whisper. "You did this to me?"

Finn's gaze never left hers. "It wasn't supposed to be like this. I thought I could protect you. But the truth is, your bloodline was never just cursed. It was a deal—a pact made long ago, and I... I was part of it. I was the one who sealed your fate."

Elara felt the earth beneath her feet shift, like the ground was crumbling away, but she stood frozen. She couldn't speak. She couldn't think. Her mind was whirling with the revelation, with the crushing weight of his words.

Behind her, she could hear the rider's voice, smooth and taunting, but it barely registered in her mind. "You see? There is no escaping the Hunt. You belong to it now, Elara. And there is no place in this world for the both of you. One of you will have to make the ultimate sacrifice."

Finn turned toward the rider, his shoulders squared, his jaw clenched tight. "No," he said, his voice firm, but Elara could hear the unspoken resignation in it. "If anyone sacrifices, it will be me."

The rider laughed, the sound dark and knowing. "You think that will save her? No. She is bound to the Hunt, and if she wants to live, she must accept her place."

Elara shook her head, her mind finally clearing enough for her to understand the gravity of what was happening. "No," she whispered, her voice breaking. "I won't let you do this. You can't make me part of it."

But the truth was already settling in, and she knew there was no turning back. She was bound to the Hunt, whether she liked it or not. And now, the greatest betrayal had come not from the Hunt, but from the one person she had trusted most—Finn.

Nine

The Choice

The air was thick with the scent of earth and moss, the deep, woody smell of ancient trees wrapping around Elara like a suffocating shroud. She felt as if the very ground beneath her was alive, pulsing with a dark energy that seemed to seep into her veins, anchoring her to the forest. The sky above was a bruised shade of purple, the last remnants of twilight fading into an oppressive night. The only light that touched the earth came from the faint, eerie glow of the rider's eyes, casting long shadows across the clearing, making everything appear distorted and unreal.

Elara could barely breathe.

Her heart hammered in her chest, each beat feeling like a drum in the silence. The words Finn had spoken were still ringing in her ears, the weight of his confession suffocating her. I was the one who bound you to the Hunt. She couldn't fathom what it meant. Couldn't understand how the man she had trusted, the one who had sworn to protect her, could have done this to her.

She was part of the Hunt, marked by it. Bound by it.

And now she had to choose.

She looked at Finn, standing a few steps away from her, his face a mask of sorrow and guilt. His eyes were dark with emotion, yet she could see the tension in his jaw, the clench of his fists at his sides. He was holding something back. She could feel it, the pull between them growing stronger, more dangerous. The desire to protect her still burned in his eyes, but there was something else—a deeper, darker knowledge that made Elara's skin crawl. He had known. He had always known what she was, what they both were.

"Elara," he said, his voice low, almost pleading. "Please, you have to understand. I never meant for it to end like this."

She wanted to scream at him, to lash out at the betrayal that had been buried deep within his words, but all she could do was stand there, frozen. The pain in her chest was unbearable, but it was nothing compared to the pull of the Hunt that was calling her, pulling her in with a force she could neither deny nor resist.

"You've known all along," she whispered, her voice trembling with a mix of fury and heartbreak. "You knew, and you still let me fall for you."

Finn's expression faltered for a moment, his eyes filled with something she couldn't name. His hand twitched at his side, as though he wanted to reach out to her, to offer some kind of comfort, but he didn't. He couldn't. The forest between them—the truth between them—had grown too thick, too tangled.

"I never wanted to hurt you," he said, his voice raw. "I didn't know how to stop it. I couldn't break the bond, Elara. I thought I could protect you, keep you away from the Hunt, but the curse… the curse was too strong."

Elara closed her eyes, trying to steady herself, but it felt as if the ground beneath her was shifting, the world spinning out of control. She wanted to say something, to accuse him of everything, but the words wouldn't come. Her throat felt tight, as though the truth had lodged itself there, choking her.

The rider—the leader of the Hunt—stepped forward, his presence heavy in the air. His eyes glowed with an eerie intensity as he watched them both, the silence stretching out like an eternity. Elara felt a cold shiver run through her, but there was no turning back now. She had to face what she had become, what they had both become.

"You are bound to us now," the rider said, his voice carrying the weight of centuries. "The price has been set. Your blood is ours. The Hunt will claim what it is owed, and there is no escape from the bond. You can no longer deny your fate, Elara."

Her heart pounded harder, faster, each beat like a drum, a countdown to the inevitable. She wanted to scream, to fight back, but the words felt distant, out of reach. She had always believed that there was a way out, that she could escape this fate, but now, standing in the clearing with the rider's eyes burning into her, she realized that escape had never been an option.

Finn moved toward her, his footsteps heavy on the ground. The air around him seemed to thrum with tension, and for a moment, Elara was lost in the magnetic pull of his presence. He had always been there for her, always fought to protect her, even when she had pushed him away. But now, standing before him, she felt something shift, something that wasn't just the weight of their past together. It was something darker.

"Don't listen to him, Elara," Finn said, his voice breaking as he reached out to her, his hand brushing against her cheek. "You don't have to choose. We can still fight this. I will fight with you."

Elara closed her eyes, his touch sending a wave of warmth through her, but it wasn't enough to drown out the cold that had settled deep within her. She knew, deep down, that Finn couldn't protect her from the Hunt, that the curse was too powerful, too ancient to fight.

She turned her face away from his touch, her heart breaking at the rawness in his eyes, the vulnerability that had been hidden beneath the walls he had built around himself. He loved her, but it wasn't enough. She had been marked by something greater, something far more dangerous than either of them could comprehend.

She swallowed hard, trying to steady her breath. "What if I don't want this?" Her voice was barely more than a whisper, but it carried the weight of everything she had ever feared. "What if I don't want to be part of the Hunt?"

The rider laughed softly, the sound like the rustling of dead leaves. "It doesn't matter what you want, Elara. The choice was made long ago. And now, you must accept the consequences."

Finn's hand shook as it fell to his side, his eyes never leaving her face. There was a sadness in them now, a depth of sorrow that Elara had never seen before. It was as though he had come to terms with the inevitability of what was happening, and it crushed her to see it.

"Elara," Finn said again, his voice hoarse. "You don't have to make this choice alone. I will stand by you, no matter what. I've always been yours."

Her heart stuttered in her chest at his words. She wanted to believe him. She wanted to hold onto the fragile thread of hope that they could somehow defy the curse, but she could feel the weight of the truth settling over her like a stone. The Hunt was part of her, part of her bloodline. There was no escape. Not for her. Not for Finn.

Her eyes flicked to the rider once more, and she knew what she had to do. She knew what choice she had to make. But the pain of it tore through her chest, a raw, jagged wound that she couldn't heal.

"I love you," she whispered, her voice barely audible over the sound of the wind rustling through the trees. "But I can't do this anymore. I can't run."

Finn's face twisted with anguish as she spoke the words, but he didn't move. He stood frozen, his body taut, his eyes wide with disbelief. The silence stretched between them, a chasm that neither of them could bridge.

The rider stepped forward then, his eyes glinting with a predatory gleam. "It is time."

Finn moved toward Elara, his hand reaching for hers one last time, but the rider was faster. A surge of dark energy filled the clearing, and before Elara could react, she felt a cold, insidious force pull her toward the rider. It was the pull of the Hunt—the call that had always been inside her, the call she had never been able to escape.

Finn's voice cracked as he shouted her name, but she was already too far gone.

Elara closed her eyes, the pain in her chest unbearable as the darkness wrapped around her, suffocating her with the weight of her fate.

Ten

Into the Abyss

The night felt colder now, the air heavy with the scent of damp earth and the faintest hint of something metallic, like blood. Elara's feet sank into the moss-covered ground as she walked, her steps slow, deliberate, but her heart racing. The moon above was a mere sliver, hidden behind a veil of dark clouds that seemed to swirl in rhythm with the pulse of the forest. It was as if the night itself was alive, breathing with the rhythm of the Hunt, and Elara felt herself caught in its undertow.

Finn had pulled away from her, though not completely. She could still feel the burn of his gaze on her, the way his presence tugged at the edge of her awareness, even as the gap between them grew wider. There was something in the air now, an unspoken tension that thrummed between them, impossible to ignore. The silence around them felt suffocating, every breath a struggle against the weight of what they were about to face.

Her hand brushed the stone wall of the ancient pathway that led deeper into the forest. The stone was cool, rough against her fingertips, as if it had been there for centuries, marking the way to some forgotten place. The sound of their footsteps was muted by the dense underbrush, the rustle of leaves and the distant hoot of an owl the only things that seemed to pierce the stillness. But that wasn't all. There was something else beneath the forest's normal sounds. A low hum, like the distant thrum of a heartbeat, reverberated through the air, as if the forest itself was breathing, waiting.

"Elara," Finn's voice broke through her thoughts, and she turned toward him. His face was shadowed, his expression unreadable. He took a step forward, his hand reaching toward her, but it faltered in the air between them. She could see the struggle in his eyes, the way he fought against whatever it was that bound him. "We can still fight this," he said, his voice low but firm.

Elara swallowed hard, her throat dry with the weight of his words. She had heard him say it before, but the truth of it felt so distant now. They had already fought, and yet here they were, standing on the edge of something far more terrifying than anything they had ever faced.

"I don't know if we can, Finn," she whispered, her voice carrying more pain than she intended. "I don't know if there's anything left to fight."

His eyes flickered, a mixture of frustration and desperation flashing across his features. He opened his mouth to speak, but she raised her hand to stop him. She couldn't hear the words anymore. Not now. They had both known, deep down, that the Hunt had already claimed her, and there was no turning back.

The rider—the leader of the Hunt—had made it clear. The bond between her bloodline and the Hunt could not be severed. And no matter how much Finn loved her, it couldn't save her from the curse that had been cast centuries ago.

Finn's shoulders slumped, and for a brief moment, Elara saw the weight of his exhaustion, the toll the journey had taken on him. She wanted to reach for him, to comfort him, but the distance between them seemed insurmountable now. Something had changed, and she didn't know if it was just the curse or the truth of their situation finally settling in.

"I can't lose you," he said softly, his voice thick with emotion. "I've already lost so much."

Elara's heart ached at the pain in his words. She had wanted to protect him, to keep him safe from the darkness that had always followed her, but now she was the one dragging them both into it. The thought of losing him—of seeing him consumed by the same fate that had claimed her—was unbearable. She took a step toward him, her hand reaching for his, but the instant her fingers brushed his skin, the world shifted.

A low, guttural sound echoed from the depths of the forest, sending a ripple of fear through her. The trees trembled, their branches creaking as if in warning, and the ground beneath her feet seemed to quake. The air grew colder, heavier, and Elara could feel the familiar pull of the Hunt's energy—the call she had always known, always fought against. But this time, it was different. This time, it was here.

Finn's grip on her tightened, pulling her closer, but the pull of the forest was stronger, like an invisible force dragging her toward the darkness that had always waited for her. She looked at him one last time, her gaze locking with his, and in that moment, she saw the truth in his eyes. He had always known this moment would come, and no matter how much he fought it, it was inevitable.

"We have to go," he whispered urgently, his voice ragged with emotion. "Now."

The urgency in his voice snapped Elara back to the present, but even as they turned to run, the ground beneath their feet shifted again. The sound of hooves echoed through the trees, their rhythmic pounding growing louder, closer. Elara's heart raced as she felt the presence of the riders closing in. She could hear the whispers now, the low chants that came from the depths of the forest, like a chorus of voices calling to her.

Finn's hand was firm around hers as they ran, but the path ahead seemed to stretch on forever, winding deeper into the heart of the forest. The trees closed in around them, their gnarled branches reaching out like fingers, pulling at the air, scraping against the sky. She could feel the walls of the forest closing in on her, and the ground beneath her feet seemed to tremble with every step they took.

"Elara," Finn called out, his voice filled with urgency. "There's a place ahead. It's the only way."

Elara's chest tightened. She wanted to ask him what he meant, but there was no time for questions. The hooves of the riders were growing louder, closer now, their sound almost deafening. She felt the pulse of their energy—dark, suffocating, like the very air around her was closing in.

Ahead, the trees parted, revealing a small clearing. In the center stood a stone altar, ancient and worn, its surface covered in moss and lichen. It was a place she had never seen before, but it felt familiar, like it was tied to her, to her bloodline, to the Hunt that had always followed her.

"This is it," Finn said, his voice barely more than a whisper.

The clearing was eerily quiet, the air still, heavy with the sense of something ancient and powerful. Elara could feel the pulse of it, the rhythm of the forest, the beat of the Hunt. She stepped forward, her heart pounding in her chest, but the moment her foot touched the ground in the clearing, everything changed.

The air crackled with dark energy, and a wave of power swept through her, washing over her skin like a cold wave. She gasped, stumbling back, but Finn was there, his arms steadying her, his face taut with fear. He looked over his shoulder, his eyes wide with recognition.

"They're here," he whispered, his voice breaking.

Elara turned, and there they were—riders emerging from the trees, cloaked in shadows, their eyes glowing with the same eerie intensity that had haunted her since the beginning. The leader of the Hunt was at the front, his eyes locked on her, a twisted smile playing on his lips.

"You cannot escape," the rider said, his voice low and commanding. "You belong to us now."

Elara's heart clenched in her chest, and for a moment, she felt the weight of her fate pressing down on her. The curse, the bloodline, the Hunt—they had all led her to this moment, to this place where she would either submit to her fate or fight for the last shred of her humanity.

Finn stepped in front of her, his body a shield, his eyes blazing with defiance. "You won't have her," he said, his voice filled with conviction. "I won't let you take her."

The rider's smile only deepened, and with a flick of his wrist, the air around them seemed to shift, darkening with an unnatural force. The forest itself seemed to lean in, the trees whispering secrets of old, secrets that Elara was only beginning to understand.

"Elara," Finn's voice broke through the tension, soft and desperate. "You don't have to do this. We can still fight. We can still—"

But the words were cut off as the rider raised his hand, his eyes burning with dark intent. "The time for fighting is over. The

Hunt has already claimed you."

Elara's breath caught in her throat, and for the first time in her life, she understood the full weight of the choice before her.

The Wild Hunt's End

The wind whipped through the trees, its mournful cry carrying across the clearing. The once-still night had erupted into a frenzy of movement, as if the very world was reacting to the gathering of the Hunt. Elara could feel the ground trembling beneath her feet, the pulse of it vibrating through her very bones. Every breath she took felt heavier, as if the air itself was thickening with the presence of the riders that surrounded them. The scent of pine and wet earth was pungent, mixing with the faint, coppery tang of something darker, something that made her stomach twist.

Her heart hammered in her chest, thudding so loudly that it drowned out everything else. The leader of the Hunt stood before her, his glowing eyes locked on hers, an unsettling smile curling beneath his hood. His presence seemed to stretch out, suffocating the space between them, casting an unnatural shadow over the clearing. His power was palpable, suffusing the air like a heavy fog, and Elara felt herself drawn to him despite every instinct screaming to turn and run.

"Elara," the rider's voice was smooth and dangerous, like the rumble of thunder before a storm. "It is time. You cannot escape what has always been yours."

Finn's hand was tight around her wrist, his touch warm but shaking, and for a brief moment, Elara thought she could feel his heart racing in time with hers. She turned to him, her gaze desperate. "Finn..." The word was barely a whisper, but it carried everything—the fear, the confusion, the love, and the haunting inevitability that neither of them could escape.

He met her eyes, his expression torn, raw. He didn't speak, but his grip on her tightened. There was nothing left to say. They were trapped.

"Do you see, Finn?" The leader's voice rang out again, cutting through the silence between them. "You were never meant to save her. She was never meant to be saved. She is mine. And you will watch as she joins us."

Elara could feel the weight of his words settling on her chest like a stone, crushing the last shreds of her resistance. The bond between her bloodline and the Hunt was not something that could be fought with mere defiance. It was an ancient curse, one as old as the very forest that surrounded them, and no matter how much she wanted to fight it, no matter how fiercely she loved Finn, the truth was inescapable.

But still, she fought. It was all she had left.

"I don't belong to you," she said, her voice hoarse but firm. "I will never belong to you."

The rider chuckled, a sound low and menacing. "Foolish girl," he murmured. "You have always belonged to the Hunt. And no matter how much you resist, you will always return to us. There is no place for you outside of this. You are a part of something greater than yourself."

His words stung, but Elara refused to let them break her. She couldn't. Not when Finn was standing beside her, not when they had fought this far to reach this point. She could feel the pull of the Hunt inside her, deep in her blood, but there was something else now—a flicker of something stronger, something that had grown between her and Finn since the very first moment their paths had crossed.

And for the first time, Elara realized what that something was.

She turned to him, the world around them blurring for a moment, the thrum of the Hunt growing louder in her ears, drowning out everything else. But she could still see Finn, still feel him, the warmth of him beside her, the urgency in his eyes. She knew, without a doubt, that he loved her—that he would never leave her. That was the force that could break this curse, the power that had always been missing.

"Finn," she said, her voice stronger now, though it trembled with the weight of what she was about to do. "I love you. And because I love you, I will fight."

His eyes softened, and for the briefest of moments, Elara saw the man she had always known—brave, unwavering, but also broken, just like her. He reached for her, his fingers brushing her cheek, and in that touch, she felt everything—the pain, the love, the shared knowledge that there was no turning back.

But it wasn't just their love that could save them. It was the bond they shared, the strength that had been forged between them, that could shatter the curse.

"I won't let them take you, Elara," Finn whispered, his voice raw. "I can't lose you. Not like this."

The air seemed to crackle around them, and for the first time, Elara felt the full force of the Hunt pressing against her. The riders closed in, their eyes glowing with anticipation, their forms flickering in and out of sight, like shadows moving in the dark. The leader stepped forward, his presence overwhelming.

"You have made your choice," the leader said, his voice ringing with finality. "Now, you will face the consequences."

Finn's grip on her tightened, but there was no fear in his eyes now—only a fierce, burning determination. "Then let the consequences come," he said, his voice steady. "Because I will stand by you, Elara. No matter what."

And in that moment, Elara felt it—an overwhelming surge of power, of love, of defiance. The forest itself seemed to respond, the air thickening with the crackle of energy, as though the ancient magic of the Hunt was being disrupted by their will. The riders faltered, their movements stuttering as though the very fabric of the curse was beginning to unravel.

"No," the leader hissed, his voice rising with fury. "This cannot be. You cannot fight what is inevitable."

But Elara and Finn were already moving. They had already made their choice. The Hunt would not claim her. Not without a fight. Not without paying the price.

With a final, desperate cry, the leader lunged toward them, but Elara was ready. She stepped forward, pulling Finn with her, and for a brief moment, the world seemed to slow. The ground beneath them seemed to shudder, the trees groaning as though the very earth was reacting to their defiance. The air around them rippled with dark energy, but Elara could feel it shifting, pushing back, as if her will—her love—was breaking through.

Finn's hand was still in hers, his pulse steady in her palm. Together, they stood against the Hunt, their love a shield against the darkness that had followed her for so long. They had made their choice. And no matter what, they would face it together.

As the leader reached out to claim them, the clearing erupted into light—bright, blinding, like the breaking of dawn. Elara squeezed Finn's hand, her heart pounding in her chest, as they stood together in the face of the storm. The Hunt had come for her. But it had not taken her. Not yet.

And for the first time in her life, Elara felt free.

Twelve

Love's Redemption

T he wind was still. The forest, which had once roared with life, was now eerily silent. The air around Elara and Finn was thick with the remnants of ancient magic, vibrating with the force of the Hunt's presence. Yet, amid it all, the clearing was strangely calm, as if the world had held its breath, waiting for something. The silence pressed down on them, heavy and suffocating, but Elara felt it differently now. She could almost hear the pulse of her own heart, the rhythmic beat of defiance in the face of the impossible.

She stood with Finn in the center of the clearing, their hands still entwined, their fingers clasped together with an intensity that felt as though they could merge into one. He was still beside her, solid and unwavering, even though the world around them seemed to crack and shift with the force of the Hunt's fury.

The riders were gone now, retreating back into the shadows from which they had emerged. The air hummed with the energy of something ancient, something that pulsed deep in the earth beneath them. But despite the unsettling quiet, Elara couldn't help but feel that they had won—at least for now.

Finn turned to her, his face illuminated only by the faint glow of the moonlight filtering through the canopy. The storm in his eyes had faded, leaving only the quiet pain of what they had both faced. His brow furrowed, his jaw tense, but his eyes, those eyes that had once been filled with uncertainty, were now steady, full of something else.

Love. Understanding.

Elara squeezed his hand tighter, her chest constricting with the emotions that flooded through her. They had come so far, and yet, in this moment, she couldn't help but wonder if they had truly broken free from the curse that had followed her family for centuries.

"Finn," she whispered, her voice trembling with the weight of everything they had just faced. "Is it over? Have we done it?"

Finn's gaze softened, his lips parting as if to answer, but he paused, the words hanging in the air between them. For a moment, Elara felt the distance between them, the space filled with so many unsaid things, so many questions left unanswered. But then, he spoke, his voice low and steady, tinged with the exhaustion of everything they had endured.

"It's over," he said simply. "The Hunt… the curse… they're gone. For you. For us."

Elara closed her eyes, a breath escaping her lips as a weight lifted from her chest. She could feel the magic in the air shifting, dissipating, like the final thread of a web being snapped. The forest, once so heavy with the presence of the Hunt, now felt lighter. Calmer.

And yet, Elara couldn't shake the feeling that something was still lingering in the shadows, waiting to pull her back. She opened her eyes, searching Finn's face for answers, but there was something else there—something she hadn't seen before, something raw and vulnerable.

"Finn," she said, her voice soft but urgent. "What did it cost? What did you sacrifice?"

His eyes darkened at the question, and for a moment, Elara thought he might pull away, might retreat behind the walls he had built so carefully. But instead, he took a deep breath, his gaze locking with hers, his hand brushing a lock of hair from her face. The air between them hummed with something both tender and devastatingly fragile.

"It cost me everything," he said, his voice a quiet rasp. "My past. My future. My very soul, if I'm being honest. But it was worth it. It was worth it for you. For us."

Elara's heart thudded painfully in her chest at his words, the weight of them settling over her like a blanket made of stones.

She had never wanted him to sacrifice himself—not for her, not for anything. But the truth of it—the depth of his love, of his devotion—was both a balm and a wound. How could she live with that? How could she live knowing that his world had been shattered for her?

"You shouldn't have had to," she whispered, her throat tight, her hand moving to his chest, her fingers trembling as they brushed the fabric of his shirt. "I never wanted you to lose yourself for me."

Finn smiled, but there was a sadness in his eyes, a resignation that twisted something deep inside her. He cupped her face gently in his hands, his touch soft but firm, as if he needed to remind himself that she was still there, still with him.

"Elara," he said, his voice tender, but laden with something more. "I would lose myself for you a thousand times over. There is nothing I wouldn't do to keep you safe. Nothing I wouldn't do to protect this."

He leaned in then, his lips brushing against hers in a kiss that was as much a promise as it was an apology. The world around them seemed to fade as they stood together in the heart of the forest, two souls bound by love and pain, by sacrifice and redemption. And for the first time in what felt like forever, Elara felt the pull of the Hunt lift from her, the weight of it dissolving into the night.

When they pulled apart, it was as if the air had changed. The clearing felt different now, less like a battleground and more like a place of renewal. The magic that had once held her captive now seemed to hum in harmony with the natural world around them, as if the forest itself had accepted their defiance.

Elara took a shaky breath, her fingers still interlaced with Finn's. "Are we free?" she asked again, her voice a whisper, barely audible over the wind that had picked up once more.

Finn nodded, a soft smile playing at the corner of his lips. "We are."

She wanted to believe him. She wanted to believe that the curse had been lifted for good, that the Hunt was nothing but a fading memory. But something in her gut told her that this was only the beginning—that whatever had bound her to this dark fate had not been fully erased. She could still feel the tendrils of it, the pull of something deep inside her, as if the forest itself was watching, waiting.

"What now?" Elara asked, her voice trembling with the uncertainty of what lay ahead. She had never imagined a life beyond the curse, a life that wasn't dictated by the weight of her bloodline's dark history. She had never known a future that wasn't shaped by the shadow of the Hunt.

Finn squeezed her hand, his expression softening. "Now we live. Together. No more running. No more hiding. Just us. And the future."

The words sounded like a dream. The kind of dream she had never allowed herself to believe in. And yet, standing there in the center of the clearing, with Finn beside her, she couldn't help but feel that it was possible. That their love—this thing that had defied the Hunt, that had defied fate itself—could be enough.

A soft rustling sound behind them caught her attention, and Elara turned, her heart leaping into her throat. The forest around them was alive again, the trees stirring in the wind, the leaves rustling with the weight of something familiar. But this time, it was different. The shadows in the forest weren't the same as before. They weren't watching them. They were welcoming them.

"I think," Finn said, his voice quiet but steady, "the forest is ready to let us go."

Elara looked around, feeling the pulse of the world around her. She could feel it now—the forest wasn't just a prison. It was a part of her. And in that moment, she knew that her past, her bloodline, her curse, had been absorbed into the very earth beneath her feet, woven into the fabric of the world around her. She was not bound to it anymore. She had become a part of something greater, something that stretched beyond the Hunt.

And in that moment, she knew that she was truly free.

As the last of the shadows disappeared into the trees, Elara turned back to Finn, her heart full. They had survived. They had fought for each other, and they had won.

And now, they could finally begin again.

www.ingramcontent.com/pod-product-compliance
Lightning Source LLC
LaVergne TN
LVHW050618200726

843508LV00010B/1909